MW01102383

THE SO[?]

and Other Stories

Nobody knows how big the universe is. Does it have an end, or does it go on for ever? Is there more than one universe? The distances in space are so great that they are measured in light-years, and who knows how many stars and planets lie beyond the reach of the eyes and ears of our science?

These stories are full of the mysteries of the universe. Why do the Tibetan lamas want to find out the nine billion names of God? What is the terrible secret discovered by scientists working on the Moon? On a far distant planet, under a different sun, Shervane knows he must cross the Wall of Darkness, even if madness lies on its other side. Bill Cross, at home on Earth, hears friendly voices in his mind; he thinks he has drunk too much whisky and does not understand the warning coming from the planet Thaar five hundred light-years away.

And on the planet Thalassa, Lora watches the starship *Magellan* as it flies in from outer space, bringing with it love and pain and dreams – the sweet sad songs of distant Earth . . .

OXFORD BOOKWORMS LIBRARY

Fantasy & Horror

The Songs of Distant Earth
and Other Stories

Stage 4 (1400 headwords)

Series Editor: Jennifer Bassett
Founder Editor: Tricia Hedge
Activities Editors: Jennifer Bassett and Christine Lindop

ARTHUR C. CLARKE

The Songs
of Distant Earth

and Other Stories

Retold by
Jennifer Bassett

OXFORD UNIVERSITY PRESS

Oxford University Press
Great Clarendon Street, Oxford OX2 6DP

Oxford New York

Athens Auckland Bangkok Bogotá Buenos Aires Cape Town
Chennai Dar es Salaam Delhi Florence Hong Kong Istanbul Karachi
Kolkata Kuala Lumpur Madrid Melbourne Mexico City Mumbai Nairobi
Paris São Paulo Shanghai Singapore Taipei Tokyo Toronto Warsaw
with associated companies in
Berlin Ibadan

OXFORD and OXFORD ENGLISH
are trade marks of Oxford University Press

ISBN 0 19 423046 5

Third impression 2001

First published in Oxford Bookworms 1996
This second edition published in the Oxford Bookworms Library 2000

Illustrated by Tony Roberts

Printed in Spain by Unigraf s.l.

CONTENTS

'This is rather unusual,' said Dr Wagner, trying very hard to hide his amazement. 'I think this must be the first time that anyone has been asked to send an Automatic Sequence Computer to a monastery in Tibet. I don't wish to seem impolite, but I do wonder what use your – er – organization has for a machine like this. Could you explain just what you plan to do with it?'

'Gladly,' replied the lama, carefully putting away his little notebook. 'Your Mark 5 Computer can do all kinds of routine mathematical work which involves up to ten figures. However, for our work we are interested in *letters*, not numbers. For this reason we wish you to change the machine so that it prints out lists of words, not figures.'

'I don't quite understand . . .'

'We have been doing this work for the last three centuries – since the monastery first began, in fact. It is a little foreign to your way of thought, so I hope you will listen with an open mind while I explain it.'

'Naturally.'

'It is really quite simple. We have been making a list which will contain all the possible names of God.'

Dr Wagner's eyes opened very wide.

'We have reason to believe,' continued the lama calmly, 'that all these names can be written with not more than nine letters in an alphabet we have invented.'

'And you have been doing this for three centuries?'

'Yes. We expected it would take us about fifteen thousand years to finish the list.'

'Oh,' Dr Wagner said slowly. 'Yes, I can see why you want one of our machines. But what exactly is your *purpose* in making this list?'

The lama hesitated for a second, and Dr Wagner wondered if the question had annoyed him. But the reply came with the same calm politeness as before.

'It is a very important part of what we believe. All the many names of the Great Being – God, Allah, Jehovah, and so on – are just names invented by humans. There are certain problems in these ideas which I do not wish to discuss here. But we believe that somewhere among all the possible arrangements of letters are what we can call the *real* names of God. By going through every possible arrangement of letters, we have been trying to list them all.'

'I see. You've been starting at AAAAAAA . . . and working through to ZZZZZZZ . . .'

'Exactly – though we use a special alphabet of our own. I'm afraid it would take too long to explain all the details, as you don't understand our language.'

'I'm sure it would,' said Dr Wagner hurriedly.

'Luckily, it will be quite easy to make the necessary changes to your Automatic Sequence Computer so that it will do this work for us and print out the names. Instead of fifteen thousand years, we shall be able to finish the list in a hundred days.'

'We have been trying to list all the real names of God.'

Dr Wagner could hear the sounds of the New York streets far below his office, but he felt that he was in a different world. High up in their distant, lonely mountains these lamas had been patiently at work, year after year, making their lists of meaningless words. Was there no end to the foolishness of human beings? But he must not show what he was thinking. The customer was always right . . .

'There's no doubt,' Dr Wagner said, 'that we can change the Mark 5 to print lists of this kind. I'm much more worried about the problems of making sure your computer is in good working condition when it arrives. And getting things out to Tibet, in these days, is not easy.'

'We can arrange that. The various parts of the computer are small enough to travel by air. If you can get them to India, we will collect them from there.'

'And you want to hire two of our engineers?'

'Yes, for the three months that the work should take.'

'There's no problem about that.' Dr Wagner wrote a note to remind himself. 'There are two more things . . .'

Before he could finish, the lama had passed him a piece of paper. 'This is from our bank and is signed, as you will see, by the manager.'

'Thank you,' Dr Wagner said, looking at the figures. 'That seems to be – er – adequate. The second question may seem a little strange, but sometimes these simple things get forgotten. There is electricity available . . .?'

'Yes, we brought in machinery for making electricity about five years ago and it works very well. It's made life at the monastery much more comfortable, but the main reason for bringing it in, of course, was to have motors to drive the prayer wheels.'

'Of course,' echoed Dr Wagner. 'Why didn't I think of that?'

*   *   *

The view from the monastery took one's breath away at first, but in time one gets used to anything. After three months, George Hanley didn't really notice the seven-hundred-metre drop, straight down into the valley below.

He was standing by the wind-smoothed stones of the low wall that ran round the outside of the main building, and staring miserably at the distant mountains. He had never been interested enough to learn their names.

This job, thought George, was the craziest thing that had ever happened to him. For weeks now the Mark 5 had been pushing out paper covered with meaningless rubbish. Patiently, endlessly, the computer had been rearranging letters in every possible way. As the sheets of paper had come out of the printers, the lamas had carefully cut them up and put them into great books. One more week, thank God, and it would be finished. George didn't know why the lamas had decided it wasn't necessary to go on to words of ten letters, or even more. His worst fear was that there would be a change of plan, and that the high lama (whom they called Sam, because it was easier than his real name) would suddenly say that the work had to go on until AD 2060.

George heard the heavy wooden door bang in the wind as Chuck came out to join him by the wall. As usual, Chuck was smoking one of the cigars that made him so popular with the lamas – who were quite willing to enjoy most of the good things in life. That was something to be thankful for, anyway. They were certainly crazy, but at least they were prepared to enjoy themselves as well.

'Listen, George,' said Chuck seriously. 'I've learned something that means trouble.'

'What's wrong? Isn't the computer behaving?' That was the worst thing that George could imagine. It might delay

*The lamas carefully cut up the sheets of paper and
put them into great books.*

his return, and nothing could be more terrible than that.
He wished desperately that he could be at home again.

'No, it's nothing like that.' Chuck sat on the low wall,
which was unusual because normally he was frightened of
the steep drop down to the valley. 'I've just learned what
all this is about.'

'What d'you mean? I thought we knew.'

'Sure. We know what the lamas are trying to do. But we didn't know *why*. It's the craziest thing—'

'Tell me something new,' said George crossly.

'—but old Sam's just told me the reason. He's getting a bit excited now that we're getting close to the end of the list. You see, they believe that when they have listed all His names – and they think that there are about nine billion of them – God's purpose in making the world will be finished. There will be nothing more for human beings to do, and indeed, no further reason for humans to go on living.'

'Then what do they expect us to do?' said George. 'All go away and kill ourselves?'

'There's no need for that. When the list's completed, God steps in and simply closes everything down . . . bang!'

'Oh, I get it. When we finish our job, it will be the end of the world.'

Chuck gave a nervous little laugh. 'That's just what I said to Sam. And do you know what happened? He looked at me in a very strange way, and said, "It's nothing as small and unimportant as *that*".'

George thought about this for a moment. 'That's what I call taking the Wide View,' he said at last. 'But what do you suppose we should do about it? I don't see that it makes any difference to us. After all, we already knew that they were crazy.'

'Yes – but don't you see what may happen? When the list's complete and God doesn't ring the final bell – or whatever it is they expect – *we* may be in trouble. It's our machine they've been using. I don't like the situation one little bit.'

'Yeah,' said George slowly, 'I see what you mean. But this kind of thing's happened before, you know. When I was a child down in Louisiana, we had a crazy churchman who once said the world was going to end next Sunday. Hundreds of people believed him – even sold their homes. But when nothing happened, they didn't get angry, as you'd expect. They just decided that he'd made a mistake in his timing, and went on believing. I guess some of them still do.'

'Well, this isn't Louisiana, in case you hadn't noticed. There are just two of us and hundreds of these lamas. I like them, and I'll be sorry for old Sam when his life's work comes to nothing. But I still wish I was somewhere else.'

'I've been wishing that for weeks. But there's nothing we can do until the job's finished and the plane arrives to fly us out.'

'Of course,' said Chuck thoughtfully, 'we could always arrange for the computer to break down.'

'Not on your life! That would make things worse.'

'No, I mean like this. The machine will finish the job four days from now, and the plane calls in a week. OK – all we have to do is to find a little problem during one of our routine checks. We'll fix it, of course, but not too quickly. If we get the timing right, we can be down at the airfield when the last name comes out of the printers. They won't be able to catch us then.'

'I don't like it,' said George. 'It will be the first time I ever walked out on a job. Anyway, they might start to suspect something. No, I'll hold on and take what comes.'

*   *   *

'I *still* don't like it,' he said, seven days later, as the tough little mountain horses carried them down the steep road. 'And don't think I'm running away because I'm afraid. I'm just sorry for those poor old men up there, and I don't want to be around when they find out how stupid they've been. I wonder how Sam will feel about it.'

'When I said goodbye to him,' said Chuck, 'I got the idea he knew we were walking out on him – and that he didn't care because he knew the computer was running smoothly and that the job would soon be finished. After that – well, of course, for him there just isn't any After That . . .'

George turned and stared back up the mountain road. This was the last place from which one could get a clear view of the monastery. The low, square buildings were dark against the evening sky; here and there, lights shone out from the narrow windows. What would happen, George wondered, when the list was finished? Would the lamas destroy the computer in their anger and disappointment? Or would they just sit down quietly and think out the problem all over again?

He knew exactly what was happening up on the mountain at this very moment. The high lama and his assistants were sitting quietly, looking carefully at the long sheets of paper as the younger lamas carried them away from the printers and put them into the great books. Nobody was speaking.

Here and there, lights shone out from the narrow windows.

The only sound was the endless noise of the printers as the computer did its work in complete silence. Three months of this, George thought, was enough to drive anyone mad.

'There it is!' called Chuck, looking down into the valley. 'Isn't that a beautiful sight!'

It certainly was, thought George. The small plane lay at the end of the airfield like a little silver cross. In two hours it would carry them away, back to the real, sensible world. It was a very comfortable thought.

Night falls quickly in the high Himalayas and darkness was already closing round them. Fortunately, the road was good and there was nothing dangerous about their journey at all. It was just very, very cold. The sky overhead was perfectly clear, and bright with the usual friendly stars. There would be no problem, thought George, about the pilot not being able to take off because of bad weather. That had been his only remaining worry.

He began to sing, but stopped after a while. His voice sounded rather small and lost among these great, silent mountains, shining like white ghosts on every side. They rode quietly on, and then George looked at his watch.

'We'll be there in an hour,' he called back over his shoulder to Chuck. Then he added, suddenly remembering, 'Wonder if the computer's finished the list. It should be just about now.'

Chuck didn't reply, so George turned his head to look back at him. He could just see Chuck's face, a white shape turned towards the sky.

'Look,' whispered Chuck, and George lifted his eyes to the sky. (There is always a last time for everything.)

Overhead, without any fuss, the stars were going out.

THE SECRET

Henry Cooper had been on the Moon for almost two weeks before he discovered that something was wrong. At first he just had a kind of strange feeling that he couldn't explain, but he was a sensible science reporter so he didn't worry about it too much.

The reason he was here, after all, was because the United Nations Space Administration had asked him to come. UNSA always liked to get sensible, responsible people to send the Moon news back to Earth. It was even more important these days, when an overcrowded world was screaming for more roads and schools and sea farms, and getting angry about all the money that was spent on space research.

So here he was, on his second visit to the Moon, and sending back reports of two thousand words a day. The Moon no longer felt strange to him, but there remained the mystery and wonder of a world as big as Africa, and still almost completely unknown. Just a stone's throw away from the enclosed Plato City was a great, silent emptiness that would test human cleverness for centuries to come.

Cooper had already visited and written about the famous place where the first men had landed on the Moon. But that now belonged to the past, like Columbus's voyage to America, and the Wright brothers, who built and flew successfully the first plane with an engine. What interested Cooper now was the future.

When he had landed at Archimedes Spaceport, everyone had been very glad to see him. Everything was arranged for his tour, and he could go where he liked, ask any questions he wanted. UNSA had always been friendly towards him because the reports and stories he sent back to Earth were accurate.

But something was wrong somewhere, and he was going to find out what it was.

He reached for the phone and said, 'Please get me the Police Office. I want to speak to the Chief Inspector.'

* * *

He met Chandra Coomaraswamy next day in the little park that Plato City was so proud of. It was early in the morning (by clock time, that is, as one Moon day was as long as twenty-eight Earth days), and there was no one around. Cooper had known the Police Chief for many years and for a while they talked about old friends and old times.

Then Cooper said, 'You know everything that's happening on the Moon, Chandra. And you know that I'm here to do a number of reports for UNSA. So why are people trying to hide things from me?'

It was impossible to hurry Chandra. He just went on smoking his pipe until he was ready to answer.

'What people?' he asked at last.

'You really don't know?'

The Chief Inspector shook his head. 'Not an idea,' he said; and Cooper knew that he was telling the truth. Chandra might be silent, but he would not lie.

'Well, the main thing that I've noticed – and it frightens

me a lot – is that the Medical Research Group is avoiding me. Last time I was here, everyone was very friendly, and gave me some fine stories. But now, I can't even meet the research boss. He's always too busy, or on the other side of the Moon. What kind of man is he?'

'Dr Hastings? A difficult man. Very clever, but not easy to work with.'

'What could he be trying to hide?'

'Oh, I'm just a simple policeman. But I'm sure a news reporter like you has some interesting ideas about it.'

'Well,' said Cooper, 'it can't be anything criminal – not in these times. So that leaves one big worry, which really frightens me. Some kind of new, killer disease. Suppose that a spaceship has come back from Mars or somewhere, carrying some really terrible disease – and the doctors can't do anything about it?'

There was a long silence. Then Chandra said, 'I'll start asking some questions. *I* don't like it either, because here's something that you probably don't know. There were three nervous breakdowns in the Medical Group last month – and that's very, very unusual.'

*   *   *

The call came two weeks later, in the middle of the night – the real Moon night. By Plato City time, it was Sunday morning.

'Henry? Chandra here. Can you meet me in half an hour at Airlock Five? Good. I'll see you there.'

This was it, Cooper knew. Airlock Five meant that they were going outside the city. Chandra had found something.

As the Moon car drove along the rough road from the city, Cooper could see the Earth, low in the southern sky. It was almost full, and threw a bright blue-green light over the hard, ugly land of the Moon. It was difficult, Cooper told himself, to see how the Moon could ever be a welcoming place. But if humans wanted to know nature's secrets, it was to places like these that they must come.

The car turned off on to another road and in a while came to a shining glass building standing alone. There was another Moon car, with a red cross on its side, parked by the entrance. Soon they had passed through the airlock, and Cooper was following Chandra down a long hall, past

Cooper could see the Earth, low in the southern sky.

laboratories and computer rooms, all empty on this Sunday morning. At last they came into a large round room in the centre of the building, which was filled with all kinds of plants and small animals from Earth. Waiting there, was a short, grey-haired man, looking very worried, and very unhappy.

'Dr Hastings,' said Coomaraswamy, 'meet Mr Cooper.' He turned to Cooper and added, 'I've persuaded the doctor that there's only one way to keep you quiet – and that's to tell you everything.'

The scientist was not interested in shaking hands or making polite conversation. He walked over to one of the containers, took out a small brown animal, and held it out towards Cooper.

'Do you know what this is?' he asked, unsmiling.

'Of course,' said Cooper. 'A hamster – used in laboratories everywhere.'

'Yes,' said Hastings. 'A perfectly normal golden hamster. Except that this one is five years old – like all the others in this container.'

'Well? What's strange about that?'

'Oh, nothing, nothing at all . . . except for the unimportant fact that hamsters live for only two years. And we have some here that are nearly ten years old.'

For a moment no one spoke, but the room was not silent. It was full of the sounds of the movements and cries of small animals. Then Cooper whispered, 'My God – you've found a way to make life longer!'

'Oh no,' Hastings said. 'We've not found it. The Moon

Dr Hastings held the hamster out towards Cooper.

has given it to us . . . and the reason has been right under our noses all the time.' He seemed calmer now, and more in control of himself. 'On Earth,' he went on, 'we spend our whole lives fighting gravity. Every step we take, every movement we make, is hard work for our bodies. In seventy years, how much blood does the heart lift through how many kilometres? But here on the Moon, where an eighty-kilo human weighs only about thirteen kilos, a body has to do only a sixth of that work.'

'I see,' said Cooper slowly. 'Ten years for a hamster – and how long for a human?'

'It's not a simple scientific law,' answered Hastings. 'It depends on a number of things, and a month ago we really didn't know. But now we're quite certain: on the Moon, a human life will last at least two hundred years.'

'And you've been trying to keep it secret!'

'You fool! Don't you understand?'

'Take it easy, Doctor – take it easy,' said Chandra softly.

Hastings took a deep breath and got himself under control again. He began to speak with icy calmness, and his words fell like freezing raindrops into Cooper's mind.

'Think of them up there,' he said, waving his hand upwards to the unseen Earth. 'Six billion of them, packed on to land which isn't big enough to hold them all. Already they're crowding over into the sea beds. And here, there are only a hundred thousand of us, on an almost empty world. But a world where we need years and years of scientific and engineering work just to make life possible; a world where only a few of the brightest and most intelligent scientists can get a job.

'And now we find that we can live for two hundred years. Imagine how they're going to feel about *that* news! This is your problem now, Mr Newsman; you've asked for it, and you've got it. Tell me this, please – I'd really be interested to know – *just how are you going to tell them?*'

He waited, and waited. Cooper opened his mouth, then closed it again, unable to think of anything to say.

In the far corner of the room, one of the baby animals began to cry.

THE WALL OF DARKNESS

Many and strange are the universes that sail like ships upon
the River of Time. Most move with the water, but some –
a very few – move against it. And just one or two lie for
ever beyond its reach, knowing nothing of the future or of
the past.

Shervane's small universe was strange in a different way.
It held one world only – the planet of Shervane's people –
and a single star, the great sun Trilorne that brought it
heat and light.

Shervane knew nothing of night, as the sun Trilorne was
always high above the horizon, dropping down closer to it
only in the long months of winter. In the Shadow Land, it
was true, there came a season when Trilorne disappeared
below the edge of the world, and a darkness fell in which
nothing could live. But even then the darkness was not
absolute.

Alone in its little universe, turning the same face always
towards its lonely sun, Shervane's world was the last and
the strangest joke of the Maker of the Stars.

As he looked across his father's lands, Shervane, like any
human child, wondered what mysteries and excitements
lay beyond the horizons. When he turned to the north,
with Trilorne shining full on his face, he could see the long
line of mountains, which ran from north to south until
they disappeared into the Shadow Land. One day, he knew,

he would cross those mountains to the great lands of the East.

To the west, not far away, was the sea, and sometimes Shervane could hear the thunder of the waves from the house. No one knew how far the sea reached. Ships had sailed northward but had always had to turn back when the heat of Trilorne became too great. Old stories spoke of the distant Fire Lands, and once, people said, there had been fast metal ships able to cross the sea even under the burning eye of Trilorne.

All the lived-in countries of Shervane's world lay in the narrow strip between burning heat and terrible cold. In every country, the far north was destroyed by the fire of Trilorne, and in the far south lay the endless, grey Shadow Land, where Trilorne was no more than a faint circle on the horizon.

All these things Shervane knew, and while he was a child, he was happy to stay in his father's wide country between the mountains and the sea. The farmland was good, and the whole land was rich in flowers and trees and clear rivers.

But time passes, even in Shervane's strange universe, and he grew older. He had learned much from his father, Sherval, but also much from his teacher, Grayle, who had taught his father and his father's father. Now the time had come for Shervane to travel east across the mountains to continue his studies.

Before he left, his father took him on a journey around his own country. They rode, on animals which we can call horses, first west, then south, until Trilorne was quite close to the horizon and it was better to turn east again. Shervane stared out across the empty Shadow Land.

'Father,' he said. 'If you went south in a straight line, right across the Shadow Land, would you reach the other side of the world?'

His father smiled. 'People have asked that question for centuries,' he said, 'and there are two reasons why they will never know the answer.'

'What are they?'

'The first, of course, is the darkness and the cold. Even here, on the edge of the Shadow Land, nothing can live during the winter months. But there is a better reason. Come – I have something to show you.'

They turned away from their route east, and for several hours rode once more with their backs to the sun. At last they came to the top of a steep hill where Sherval stopped and pointed to the far south.

'It is not easy to see,' he said quietly. 'My father showed it to me from this same hill, many years before you were born.'

Shervane stared into the shadowy distance. The southern sky was dark, almost black, and it came down to meet the edge of the world. But not quite black, because along the horizon, between the land and the sky but belonging to neither, was a line of deeper darkness, black as the night which Shervane had never known.

He stared at it for a long time, and after a while he suddenly felt that the darkness was alive and waiting. He

Along the horizon, between the land and the sky,
was a line of deeper darkness.

did not understand this feeling, but he knew that nothing
would ever be the same again.

And so, for the first time in his life, Shervane saw the
Wall.

*   *   *

In the early spring he said goodbye to his people and travelled over the mountains into the great lands of the eastern world. Here he continued his studies, and in the places of learning he made friends with boys who had come from lands even farther to the east. One of these boys, Brayldon, was studying to be an architect, and he and Shervane spent many hours discussing their ideas and dreams for the future.

Between them they took the world to pieces and rebuilt it to their own plan. Brayldon dreamed of cities whose wide streets and beautiful buildings would be the wonders of the world, but Shervane was more interested in the people who would live in these cities, and how they would order their lives.

They often spoke of the Wall, which Brayldon knew about but had never seen. Far to the south of every country, rising huge and black into the grey sky, the Wall ran in an unbroken line across the Shadow Land, never pausing even when it reached the sea. Travellers on those lonely coasts had reported how the dark shadow of the Wall marched out into the waves and beyond the horizon. In summer it was possible to make the journey to the Wall, though only with difficulty, but nowhere was there any way of passing it, and no one knew what lay beyond.

'One of my uncles,' said Brayldon, 'reached the Wall when he was a young man. He rode for ten days before he came beneath it. I think it frightened him – it was so huge and cold. He could not tell whether it was made of metal or stone, and when he shouted, his voice died away at once and there was no echo at all. My people believe it is the end of the world, and there is nothing beyond.'

'*My* people believe it was built by men,' said Shervane, 'perhaps by the engineers of the First Age, who made so many wonderful things – even, people say, ships that could fly.'

'That may be true,' said Brayldon, 'but we will still never know *why* they built it, or what lies beyond it.'

But Shervane could not accept that there were no answers to these questions, and he went on asking them. Before he came east, Grayle, his old teacher at home, had told him:

'There is only one thing beyond the Wall, so I have heard. And that is madness.'

Artex, one of the great teachers in the east, had given Shervane a different answer:

'The Maker built the Wall in the third day of making the world. What is beyond, we shall discover when we die, as that is where the dead go.'

But Irgan, who lived in the same city, gave a different answer again:

'Behind the Wall is the land where we lived before we were born. If we could remember that far back, we would know the answers to your questions.'

Shervane did not know who to believe. The truth was that no one knew the answers, and perhaps had never known.

Soon Shervane's year of study came to an end. He said goodbye to Brayldon and began the long, dangerous journey home across the great mountains, where walls of ice rose high into the sky. As he came to the last and highest part of the road, he could see, far below in the valley, the line of shadow that was his own country. He went on down to the last bridge, looking forward to his homecoming and journey's end.

But the bridge was gone, destroyed by the storms and rockfalls of early spring, and now lay in pieces in the river three hundred metres below. It would take a year to rebuild it, Shervane realized sadly, and he turned his horse and rode back to the east.

*   *   *

Brayldon was still in the city when Shervane returned. He was surprised and pleased to see his friend again, and together they made plans for the year ahead.

It was Shervane's idea, and though many people shook their heads doubtfully and advised them not to do it, by summer the two friends were ready to begin their journey. First they rode east, to lands that Brayldon knew, then turned south and rode, for day after day, across the grey Shadow Land. The Wall never seemed to get any nearer, and it was only when they were standing at its foot, staring up at its huge, endless blackness, that they realized they had arrived.

It was even stranger than travellers' stories had prepared them for. It felt neither hard nor soft, and was cold – too cold, even for something in a land untouched by the sun. Strangest of all was the silence: every word, every sound died away with unnatural quickness.

Brayldon took out some tools, but he soon found that nothing could cut or even mark the Wall's surface in any way. The Wall was not just hard; it was almost untouchable. At last Brayldon took out a perfectly straight piece of metal and held its edge hard against the Wall, but when he looked carefully along the line of contact, a very narrow line of light showed unbroken between the two surfaces.

Brayldon looked thoughtfully at his friend.

'Shervane,' he said. 'I don't believe the Wall is made of anything known to our science.' He put away his useless cutting tools and took out a theodolite. 'If I can do nothing else,' he said with a smile, 'at least I can find out how high it is!'

When they rode away and looked back for their last view of the Wall, Shervane decided that there was nothing more he could learn. He must forget this foolish dream, this wish to find out the Wall's secret. Perhaps there was

no secret at all. Perhaps beyond the Wall the Shadow Land just continued round the curve of the world until it met the same Wall again on the other side. But then why . . .?

Angrily, he put it out of his mind and rode north into the light of Trilorne.

* * *

When Shervane took the road across the mountains again, he had been away for two years and he was full of happiness to be going home again. As he rode down into the valley, he saw a line of horsemen coming towards him, and he hurried on, hoping that his father Sherval had come to meet him.

But it was Grayle who rode up to him, and put his hand on Shervane's shoulder, then turned his head away, unable to speak.

As Shervane rode down into the valley, he saw
a line of horsemen coming towards him.

And presently Shervane learned that the storms of the year before had destroyed more than the mountain bridge. The lightning in that storm had hit his home, burning the great house to the ground and killing all his family in one terrible night.

In a single moment of time all the land had passed to Shervane, and he was now the richest man his country had known. But it meant nothing to Shervane. He would give everything, he thought, to look again into the calm grey eyes of the father he would see no more.

*   *   *

Years passed and Trilorne rose and fell in the sky many times before Shervane thought again of the Wall. He had taken good care of all his farms and land, and now he had time once more in which to dream. More than that – he had the riches to make his dreams come true. And what was the use of riches unless they could be used to shape one's dreams?

So Shervane wrote to Brayldon, now an architect famous in many lands for his wonderful buildings, and asked him to join in his old friend's dream – and his plan.

Early the next summer Brayldon came and the two men were soon deep in discussions, studying the drawings and the architect's plans that Brayldon had already prepared. Before Shervane finally decided, he took his friend to see Grayle.

Grayle was now very old but his advice was always ready when it was needed, and it was always wise. Brayldon put out the plans and drawings, and Grayle studied them in silence. The largest drawing showed the Wall, with a great stairway rising along its side from the ground beneath. At six places on the stairway there was a wide platform; the last one was only a short distance below the top of the Wall.

At last Grayle spoke. 'I always knew you would want to do something like this one day, Shervane. But how much will it cost?'

Brayldon told him, and the old man's eyes opened wide in surprise.

'That's because,' the architect said quickly, 'we have to build as well a road across the Shadow Land and a small town for the workmen to live in during the building of the stairway. We will have to make our own building materials in the Shadow Land, you see; it would be even more expensive to carry them across the mountains.'

Grayle looked more closely at the drawing. 'Why have you stopped short of the top?'

'I want to be the only one to go all the way up,' replied Shervane. 'There will be a lifting machine on the highest platform. There may be danger; that is why I am going alone.'

It was not the only reason, but it was a good one. Behind the Wall, so Grayle had once said, lay madness. If that were true, no one else need face it.

'That is good,' said Grayle quietly. 'If the Wall was built to keep something from our world, it will still be impassable from the other side.'

'And,' added Brayldon, 'we can, if necessary, destroy the

stairway in seconds by explosives already built in at certain places.'

*   *   *

It was seven years before the last stones were in place on the great stairway. Work could only continue during the summer months while Trilorne was above the horizon, and there was always the worry that the winter storms would destroy the work of the summer before. But Brayldon had built well and each year the stairway grew slowly higher.

At last came the time when Shervane knew that his dream would soon become real. Standing two kilometres away, so that he could see the whole stairway, he remembered the day when, as a boy at his father's side, he had first seen the Wall and felt it was alive and waiting for him.

The top platform was so high above the ground that Shervane did not care to go near its edge. With Brayldon's help, he got into the lifting machine that would take him the last ten metres to the top, then turned to his friend.

'I shall only be gone a few minutes,' he said, more calmly than he felt. 'Whatever I find, I'll return immediately.'

How could he guess that there would be little for him to choose or decide?

*   *   *

Grayle's eyesight had almost gone during the seven years of building, but his hearing was still sharp and he recognized Brayldon's footsteps before his visitor had time to speak.

'Ah, Brayldon, I'm glad you came,' he said. 'I've been thinking of everything you have told me about the Wall, and I believe I know the truth at last.' He paused for a moment. 'Perhaps you have guessed it already.'

'No,' said Brayldon. 'I have been afraid to think of it.'

The old man smiled a little.

'Why should one be afraid of something just because it is strange? The Wall is wonderful, yes – but there is no need to fear it, for those who understand its secret.

'So many stories have been told about the Wall, Brayldon. But I think I can now see the ones that are true. Long ago, during the First Age, Trilorne was hotter than it is now and it was possible to live and farm in the Shadow Land. People could go as far southward as they wanted, because there was no Wall to stop them. What happened to Shervane happened to them also, and so the scientists of the First Age built the Wall to stop people going mad. Stories say – though I cannot believe this – that the Wall was built in a single day, out of a cloud that encircled the world.'

He fell silent, and for a moment Brayldon was silent too, trying to imagine that distant world of the past.

* * *

As the lifting machine took him up to the top of the Wall, Shervane tried to bury his fear deep inside him. But it was hard. What if, after all, the Wall *had* been built to keep some horror from the world? Then, suddenly, he was there, staring out at something he did not at first understand.

Then he realized that he was looking across an unbroken black sheet, which disappeared into the distance. He stepped onto the Wall and began to walk carefully forward, keeping his back to Trilorne.

There was something wrong: it was growing darker with

Shervane stepped onto the Wall and began to walk carefully forward.

every footstep he took. Afraid, he turned around and saw that Trilorne had now become faint and shadowy, like a light seen through a darkened glass. Then his fear grew greater, as he realized that was not all – *Trilorne was smaller than the sun he had known all his life.* He shook his head angrily; he was imagining it. A thing like that couldn't possibly be true. He walked on bravely, with only the occasional look at the sun behind him.

Soon the darkness was all around him, and Trilorne had almost disappeared, leaving only a faint light in the sky to mark its place. A wise man would turn back now, he thought, but still he went on.

Then he saw, far ahead of him, a second light appearing in the sky. Behind him, Trilorne had now disappeared completely, but as he walked on, he saw that this new light was another sun, growing bigger by the minute, just as Trilorne had grown smaller. Amazement took hold of him. Did his world have two suns, one shining on it from either side?

Now at last he could see, faintly through the darkness, the black line that marked the Wall's other edge. Soon he would be the first man in thousands of years, perhaps ever, to look upon the lands on the other side of the wall. Would there be people in those lands, and what kind of people would they be?

He had no idea – how could he? – who they were, and that they were waiting for him.

*   *   *

Grayle put out his hand to the table beside him and found

a large piece of paper that was lying on it. Brayldon watched him in silence, and the old man continued.

'People have always argued about the universe – how big it is, where it ends, whether it ends at all, or goes on for ever. It is difficult for our minds to imagine something that has no end. There have been many answers given to these questions, and some of them may be true of other universes – if there *are* other universes – but for our universe the answer is rather different.

'*Along the line of the Wall, Brayldon, our universe comes to an end – and yet does not.* Before the Wall was built, there was nothing to prevent people going onwards. The Wall itself is only a man-made thing, but it has the same strangeness as the space it now fills.'

He held the piece of paper towards Brayldon and slowly turned it round and round.

'Here,' he said, 'is a simple piece of paper. It has, of course, two sides. *Can you imagine one that has not?*'

Brayldon stared at him in amazement.

'That's impossible – quite impossible!'

'But is it?' said Grayle softly. On the table his hand searched for and found a long, thin strip of paper. He ran his fingers along the paper strip, then joined the two ends together so that the strip had the shape of a circle.

'The scientists of the First Age,' he went on, 'had minds that could understand this fully, but this simple example may help to show you the truth. Watch. I run my finger around the inside, so – and now along the outside. The two surfaces are quite separate; you can go from one to the other only by moving through the thickness of the strip. Do you agree?'

'Of course,' said Brayldon, still puzzled. 'But what does it prove?'

'Nothing,' said Grayle. 'But now watch . . .'

*   *   *

This sun, Shervane thought, was exactly the same as Trilorne. The darkness had now lifted completely, and he no longer had the feeling that he was walking endlessly into nothingness. He began to walk more slowly, afraid of coming too suddenly to the Wall's edge, and in a while he could see a distant horizon of low hills, as grey and lifeless as those he had left behind. But he was not disappointed; the Shadow Land of his own world would look no better than this.

So he walked on. And when presently an icy hand fastened itself upon his heart, he did not pause or show any sign of fear. He went bravely on, watching the land in front of him, until he could see the place where his journey had started, and the great stairway itself, and at last Brayldon's worried, waiting face.

*   *   *

Again Grayle brought the two ends of the paper strip together, but now he had given it a half-turn so that the circle of paper had a twist in it. He held it out to Brayldon.

'Run your finger around it now,' he said quietly.

Brayldon did not do so; he could see the old man's meaning.

'I understand,' he said. 'You no longer have two separate

surfaces. It is now a single continuous piece of paper – *a one-sided surface* – something that at first sight seems quite impossible.'

'Yes,' said Grayle softly. 'I thought you would understand. A *one-sided surface*. Of course, a piece of paper only has *two* dimensions, but it gives us a simple example of what must happen, in *three* dimensions, at the Wall.'

There was a long silence. Then Grayle spoke again:

'Why did you come back before Shervane?' he asked, though he knew the answer well enough.

'We had to do it,' said Brayldon sadly, 'but I did not wish to see my work destroyed.'

'I understand,' said Grayle kindly.

*   *   *

Shervane looked up and down the great stairway on which no feet would ever step again. He did not feel sad; he had learnt, as much as it was possible to learn.

Slowly he lifted his hand and gave the sign. The explosion seemed to make no sound at all, and the stones of the great stairway flew outwards and began to fall in a calm, unhurried way that Shervane would remember all his life. For a moment there came into his mind a picture of another stairway, watched by another Shervane, falling in just the same slow, gentle way on the far side of the Wall.

But that, he realized, was a foolish thought; as no one knew better than he that the Wall had no other side.

For a moment there came into his mind a picture of another stairway.

'But this is terrible!' said the Great Scientist. 'Surely there is *something* we can do!'

'Yes, Your Highness, but it will be extremely difficult. The planet is more than five hundred light-years away, and it is hard to make contact. However, we believe we can do it, but there is another problem. So far, we have been quite unable to communicate with these people – they do not seem to be telepathic in any way. And if we cannot talk to them, we cannot help them.'

There was a long silence while the Great Scientist thought about the problem, and arrived, as he always did, at the right answer.

'Any intelligent beings must have *some* telepathic people among them. We must send out hundreds of searchers, ready to catch the smallest thought. When you find a single open mind, work as hard as you can on it. We *must* get our message through.'

'Very good, Your Highness. We will begin at once.'

Across the huge emptiness of space, which light itself took half a thousand years to cross, the brains of the planet Thaar sent out their long lines of thought, searching desperately for a single human being whose mind could receive their message. And they were lucky – they found Bill Cross.

At least, they thought it was luck at the time, though

later they were not so sure. And it was only chance that opened Bill's mind to them for a few seconds – a chance that was not likely to happen again for many centuries.

There were three reasons for this chance happening. First, at that moment in the Earth's movement around its sun, Bill was well placed to receive a message from Thaar. So, of course, were millions of other people on the same part of the Earth's surface, but then they were not rocket engineers; they had not spent years thinking and dreaming about space and space travel.

And they were not, as Bill was, very, very drunk, on the edge of unconsciousness, trying to escape from reality into the world of dreams, where there were no disappointments.

Of course, Bill could understand the army's opinion.

'You are paid, Dr Cross,' his boss had told him sharply, 'to make rockets which can carry bombs. You are *not* paid to invent spaceships, or to use the computers here for your own purposes. So this must now stop.'

Bill knew that he wouldn't lose his job; he was too valuable to the army for that. But did he want the job anyway? He wasn't sure of anything except that he felt angry and miserable – and that Brenda had finally gone off with Johny Gardner.

He put his chin in his hands, stared dully at the white wall on the other side of the table, and emptied his mind of thought . . .

At that moment, several thousand brains on Thaar gave a soundless cry of delight, and the wall in front of Bill disappeared into a kind of mist. He seemed to be looking down a tunnel that had no end. And in fact, he was.

Bill stared at it with interest, but he was used to seeing hallucinations when he was drunk, and he had seen more exciting ones than this. And when the voice started to speak in his mind, he did not reply at first. Even when drunk, he didn't like having conversations with himself.

'Bill,' the voice began, 'listen carefully. We have had great difficulty contacting you, and this is extremely

The wall in front of Bill disappeared into a kind of mist.

important. We are speaking to you from a very distant planet. You are the only human being we have been able to contact, so you *must* understand what we are saying.'

Bill felt a little worried. How serious was it, he wondered, when you started to hear voices? Well, it was best not to get excited.

'OK,' he said, sounding bored. 'Go ahead and talk to me. I won't mind – if it's interesting.'

There was a pause. Then the voice continued, still in a friendly way, but now rather worried as well.

'But our message isn't just *interesting*. It means life or death for all human beings.'

'I'm listening,' said Bill. 'It'll help to pass the time.'

Five hundred light-years away, the Thaarns talked hurriedly among themselves. Something seemed to be wrong, but they could not decide exactly what. They had certainly made contact, but this was not the kind of reply they had expected. Well, they could only carry on and hope for the best.

'Listen, Bill,' they continued. 'Our scientists have just discovered that your sun is going to explode three days from now – in seventy-four hours, to be exact. Nothing can stop it. But don't be alarmed. We can save you, if you do what we say.'

'Go on,' said Bill. This hallucination was certainly unusual.

'We can make what we call a bridge – it's a kind of tunnel through space, like the one you're looking into now. It's difficult to explain, even to one of your mathematicians.'

'Just a minute,' argued Bill. 'I *am* a mathematician, and a good one, drunk or not drunk. I suppose you're talking about some kind of short cut through a higher dimension of space. That's an old idea – before Albert Einstein.'

A feeling of surprise entered Bill's mind.

'We had no idea you knew so much about science,' said the Thaarns. 'But there's no time to discuss that. The important thing is this – if you stepped into that tunnel in front of you, you'd find yourself immediately on another planet. It's a short cut, as you said, but through the thirty-seventh dimension.'

'And it leads to your world?'

'Oh no – you couldn't live here. But there are plenty of planets like Earth in the universe, and we've found one that will suit human beings. We'll make bridges like this all over Earth, so your people can just walk through them and escape. They'll have to start from the beginning on the new planet, of course, but it's their only hope. You must pass on this message, and tell them what to do.'

'But no one's going to listen to me,' Bill said. 'Why don't you talk to the president?'

'Because yours was the only mind we could contact. Others seemed closed to us; we don't understand why.'

'I could tell you,' said Bill, looking at the empty whisky bottle in front of him. He was really enjoying this hallucination, though it was easy to explain it. Only last week he'd been reading a story about the end of the world. But how good was this hallucination on details?

'If the sun does explode,' he asked, 'what will happen?'

'Your planet will be destroyed at once. All the planets, in fact, right out to Jupiter.'

Rather a fine disaster, Bill thought. And the more he thought about it, the more he liked it.

'My dear hallucination,' he said kindly, 'if I believed you—'

'But you *must* believe us!' came the worried cry across the light-years.

'I'd say *it would be a very good thing*,' Bill went on happily. 'Yes, it would save a lot of misery. No more worries about bombs, and people killing each other, or not having enough food to eat. Oh, it would be wonderful. Nice of you to come and tell us, but you can just go back home and take all your old bridges with you.'

There was great alarm and amazement on Thaar. The Great Scientist's brain, swimming like a huge piece of rock in its bath of liquid food, turned yellow at the edges, and the main computer in the College of Higher Mathematics burnt itself out in a quarter of a second.

And on Earth, Bill Cross still hadn't finished.

'Look at *me*,' he said. 'I've spent years trying to make rockets do something useful, and they tell me I'm only allowed to make rockets for bombs, so that we can all blow each other up. The sun will make a better job of it, and if you did give us another planet, we'd only do the same stupid things all over again. And,' he went on sadly, 'Brenda's left town without even writing a note to say goodbye. So you see, I'm not very enthusiastic about your kind offer of help.'

In a final desperate attempt, the Thaarns sent their thoughts along the tunnel between the stars.

'You can't really mean it, Bill! Are *all* human beings like you?'

Bill considered this question carefully. The whisky was beginning to make him feel much happier. After all, things could be worse. Perhaps he would look for another job. As for Brenda – well, women were like buses; there'd always be another one along in a minute. And best of all, there was a second bottle of whisky in the cupboard. He got to his feet and walked drunkenly across the room to get it.

For the last time, Thaar spoke to Earth.

'Bill!' it repeated desperately. 'Surely all human beings can't be like you!'

Bill turned and looked into the misty tunnel. It seemed to have starlight shining in it, and was really rather pretty. He felt proud of himself; not many people could imagine *that*.

'Like me?' he said. 'No, they're not.' The whisky swam happily through his brain. 'I suppose I'm one of the lucky ones, really,' he said.

Then he stared in surprise, as the tunnel had suddenly disappeared and the wall was there again, exactly as it had been. Thaar knew when it was beaten.

'I was getting tired of that hallucination, anyway,' Bill thought. 'Let's see what the next one's like.'

But there wasn't a next one, because five seconds later Bill fell down unconscious, just as he was trying to open the second bottle of whisky.

The tunnel seemed to have starlight in it,
and was really rather pretty.

For the next two days he felt rather ill and he forgot all about the strange conversation through the tunnel. On the third day he felt there was something he ought to remember, but then Brenda came back to him and there were lots of tears and kisses, and he didn't have time to think about it.

And there wasn't a fourth day, of course.

Beneath the trees Lora waited, watching the sea. She could just see Clyde's boat on the horizon, and soon it grew bigger and bigger as it came quickly over the calm blue water towards her.

'Where are you, Lora?' Clyde's voice asked crossly from the wrist radio he had given her when she agreed to marry him. 'Come and help me – we've got a lot of fish to bring home.'

So! Lora thought; *that's* why he asked me to hurry down to the beach. To punish him a little, she did not reply to his repeated calls on the radio, but when his boat arrived, she came out from the shadows under the great trees and walked slowly down the beach to meet him.

Clyde jumped out, smiling, and gave Lora a big kiss. Together, they began to empty the boat of its many kilos of fish. They were not true fish, of course; in the sea of this young planet it would be a hundred million years before nature made real fish. But they were good enough to eat, and they were called by the old names that the first colonists had brought with them from Earth.

Soon Clyde and Lora were driving the catch home, but they had made only half the short journey when the simple, carefree world they had known all their young lives came suddenly to its end.

High above them, they heard a sound their world had

not known for centuries – the thin scream of a starship coming in from outer space, leaving a long white tail like smoke across the clear blue sky.

Clyde and Lora looked at each other in wonder. After three hundred years of silence, Earth had reached out once more to touch Thalassa . . .

Why? Lora asked herself. What had happened, after all these years, to bring a starship from Earth to this quiet peaceful world? There was no room for more colonists here on Thalassa, and Earth knew that well enough. It was a young planet – still only a single large island in a huge, encircling sea. In time new land would rise up out of the sea, but not for many millions of years.

When the first colonists came to Thalassa, they had worked hard to make a new life – making farms and growing food, building towns and factories. In later years, with rich farming land and seas full of fish, the colonists' descendants enjoyed an easy, comfortable life. They worked as much as necessary (but no more), happy to dream fondly of Earth, and to let the future take care of itself.

When Lora and Clyde arrived back at the village, there was great excitement. The starship, people said, seemed to be coming in to land, and it would probably come down in the hills where the first colonists had landed.

Soon everybody who could find a bicycle or a car was moving out of the village on the road to the west. Lora's father, who was the Mayor of Palm Bay village with its 572 people, proudly led the way, silently repeating to himself suitable words of welcome for the visitors.

The ship came in silently, with no sound of engines, and landed softly on the green grass. It looked, thought Lora, like a great silver egg, waiting to bring something new and strange into the peaceful world of Thalassa.

'It's so small!' someone whispered behind her. 'Did they come from Earth in *that* thing?'

'Of course not,' someone whispered back. 'That's only a little space bus. The real starship's up there in space—'

'Sshh! They're coming out!'

One moment the sides of the silver egg were smooth and unbroken; and then, a second later, there was a round doorway, with steps coming down to the ground. Then the visitors appeared, shading their eyes against the bright light of a new sun. There were seven of them – all men – tall and thin, with white faces.

It looked like a great silver egg.

They came down to the ground and Lora's father stepped forward. Words of welcome were spoken, hands were shaken, but Lora saw and heard none of it, because in that moment, she saw Leon for the first time.

He came out of the ship a little after the other seven – a man with deep, dark eyes in a strong face, eyes that had looked on sights that Lora could not even imagine. He was not handsome, and his face looked serious, even worried, but Lora knew a feeling of both fear and wonder, a feeling that her life would never be the same again.

He looked around the crowd and saw Lora. Their eyes locked together, bridging time and space and experience. The worry slowly disappeared from Leon's face; and presently, he smiled.

*   *   *

It was late evening by the time all the welcoming parties had finished. Leon was very tired, but he could not sleep; his mind was still too busy with the problems of the starship. After the worry of the last few weeks, when he and the other engineers had been woken by the scream of alarm bells and had fought to save the wounded starship, it was hard to realize that they were safe at last. What luck that this planet had been so close! Now they could probably repair the ship and complete the two centuries of travelling that still lay before them. And if not, they would be able to find a new home here, among people of their own kind.

The night was cool and calm, and the sky bright with unknown stars. Still too restless to sleep, Leon left the simple resthouse that had been prepared for the visitors and walked out into the single street of Palm Bay. The villagers all seemed to be in bed and asleep, which suited Leon, who wanted only to be left alone until he felt ready to sleep.

In the quietness of the night he could hear the soft whisper of the sea, and he left the street and turned his steps towards the beach. Soon he was under the dark shadows of trees, but the smaller of Thalassa's two moons was high in the south and its thin yellow light was enough to show him the way. He came out from the trees on to the beach and stood looking at the fishing boats along the water's edge. For a moment he wished he was not a starship engineer, but could enjoy the simple, peaceful life of a fisherman on this quiet planet.

He put the dream quickly out of his mind and began to walk along by the sea's edge, and as he walked, Selene, the second moon, rose above the horizon, filling the beach with golden light.

And in that sudden brightness, Leon saw that he was not alone.

The girl was sitting on one of the boats, about fifty metres further along the beach, and staring out to sea. Leon hesitated. She was probably waiting for someone; perhaps he should turn quietly back to the village.

He had decided too late, because then the girl looked up and saw him. Unhurriedly, she rose to her feet, and Leon walked slowly on towards her. He stopped a few metres away from her and smiled.

'Hello,' he said. 'I was just taking a late walk – I hope I haven't frightened you.'

'Of course not,' Lora answered, trying to keep her voice calm and expressionless. She could not really believe that she was doing this – meeting a complete stranger on a lonely beach at night. All day she had been unable to put the young engineer out of her mind. She had found out his name, had watched and planned, and hurried to the beach ahead of him when she saw him leave the resthouse and walk towards the trees. Now she felt suddenly afraid, but it was too late to turn back.

Leon began to speak again, then stopped, suddenly recognizing her and realizing what she was doing here. This was the girl who had smiled at him when he came out of the ship – no, that was not right; *he* had smiled at *her* . . .

They stared at each other wordlessly, wondering what strange chance of time and space had brought them together.

This is crazy, Leon told himself. What am I doing here? I should apologize and go – and leave this girl to the peaceful world that she has always known.

But he did not leave. 'What's your name?' he said.

'I'm Lora,' she answered, in the soft voice of the islanders.

'And I'm Leon Carrell, Assistant Rocket Engineer, Starship *Magellan*.'

She smiled a little and he saw at once that she already knew his name. Then she spoke again:

'How long do you think you will be here, on Thalassa?'

'I'm not sure,' he replied, truthfully enough. He could see that his answer was important to her. 'It depends how long it takes to do our repairs. We have to make a new starship shield, you see, as the old one was destroyed when something big hit us out in space.'

'And you think you can make a new one here?'

'We hope so. The main problem is how to lift about a million tonnes of water up to the *Magellan*.'

'Water?' Lora looked puzzled. 'I don't understand.'

'Well, you know that a starship travels through space at almost the speed of light. Unfortunately, space is full of bits and pieces of rock and other things, and at that speed anything that hits us would burn up the ship immediately. So we carry a shield about a kilometre ahead of us, and let *that* get burned up instead.'

'And you can make a new one out of *water*?'

'Yes. It's the cheapest building material in the universe. We freeze it into a huge piece of ice that travels ahead of us. What could be simpler than that?'

Lora did not answer, and seemed to be thinking of something else. Presently she said, a little sadly:

'And you left Earth a hundred years ago.'

'A hundred and four. It seems like only a few weeks because we were deep-sleeping until the alarms woke us engineers. The ship is flown by automatic controls, of course, and all the other colonists are still in suspended animation. They don't know that anything has happened.'

'And soon you'll join them again, and sleep your way on to the stars for another two hundred years.'

'That's right,' said Leon, not looking at her.

Lora looked round at the island behind them. 'It's strange to think that your sleeping friends up there will never know anything of all this. I feel sorry for them.'

'Yes, only we fifty engineers will remember Thalassa.'
He looked at Lora's face and saw sadness in her eyes. 'Why
does that make you unhappy?'

Lora shook her head, unable to answer. She felt a great
loneliness, a horror at the huge emptiness of space and that
three-hundred-year journey through the emptiness. Suddenly
she wanted to be at home, in her own room, in the world
she knew and understood. She wished she had never come
on this mad adventure – and she thought of Clyde, and felt
ashamed.

'What's the matter?' asked Leon. 'Are you cold?' He
held out his hand to her and their fingers touched, but she
pulled her hand away at once.

Leon held out his hand to her and their fingers touched.

'It's late,' she said, almost angrily. 'I must go home. Goodbye.'

She turned and walked quickly away, leaving Leon staring after her, puzzled and a little hurt. What had he said to annoy her? Then he called after her:

'Will I see you again?'

If she answered, the words were lost in the noise of the sea, but Leon knew, as surely as the sun would rise tomorrow, that they would meet again.

*   *   *

The life of the island now centred around the huge wounded starship two thousand kilometres out in space. In the early morning and late evening, the *Magellan* could be seen as a bright star in the sky above. And even when it could not be seen, people were thinking and talking about it. It was the most exciting thing that had happened to Thalassa in centuries.

The starship's engineers seemed to be busy all the time, hurrying around the island, digging deep holes in the ground to study the rocks, using strange scientific tools that the islanders had never seen before. Most people, in fact, had no idea at all what the engineers were doing, and the engineers, although friendly, had no time to explain.

It was two days before Lora spoke to Leon again. From time to time she saw him as he hurried around the village, but they were only able to smile at each other in passing. But this was enough to make Lora's heart beat wildly, and to make her sharp and unfriendly with Clyde. She had been so sure that she loved Clyde, and would marry him. Now she was not sure of anything, except her desperate, burning wish to be with Leon every minute of the day. Why this had happened to her, she did not know. She knew only that she had fallen in love with a man who had come into her life from nowhere, and who must leave again in a few weeks.

By the end of the first day, only her family knew about her feelings; by the end of the second day, everyone she passed gave her a knowing smile. It was impossible in a small place like Palm Bay to keep anything secret.

Her second meeting with Leon was in the Mayor's office. Lora was helping her father with the paperwork that the Earthmen's visit had caused when the door opened and Leon walked in, asking to see the Mayor. Lora's younger sister hurried away to fetch him, and Leon sat tiredly down in a chair by the door. Then he saw Lora watching him silently from the other side of the room, and jumped to his feet.

'Hello – I didn't know you worked here.'

'I live here. My father's the Mayor.'

Leon walked over to her desk and picked up a book that was lying there. He said something about it and Lora replied politely, but there were unspoken questions in her mind. When can we meet again? And does he really like me, or is he just making polite conversation?

Then the Mayor hurried in to see his visitor, who had brought a message from the starship's captain. Lora pretended to work but she understood not one word of the papers she was reading.

When Leon had left, the Mayor walked over to his daughter and picked up some of the papers on her desk.

'He seems a nice young man,' he said, 'but is it a good idea to get too fond of him?'

'I don't know what you mean,' said Lora.

'Now, Lora! I *am* your father, and I do have *eyes* in my head, you know.'

'He's not' – and here Lora's voice shook a little – 'a bit interested in me.'

'Are you interested in him?'

'I don't know. Oh, Daddy, I'm so unhappy!'

The Mayor was not a brave man, so there was only one thing he could do. He gave Lora his handkerchief, and ran back into his office.

*   *   *

It was the most difficult problem that Clyde had ever had in his life. Lora belonged to him – everyone knew that. With another villager, or a man from any other part of Thalassa, Clyde knew exactly what he would do. And because Clyde was a tall, strong young man, there had never been any trouble at those other times when he had politely advised the man to leave his girl alone. But Leon was an Earthman, an important visitor. It was not easy to offer that kind of advice to him, however politely.

During his long hours at sea, Clyde played with the idea of a short, sharp fight with Leon. But he knew that he was stronger than the Earthman, so it wouldn't be a fair fight.

And anyway, was he really sure that he had a reason to fight Leon? It was true that Leon seemed to be at the

Mayor's house every time that Clyde called, but that could mean everything – or nothing. Jealousy was new to Clyde, and he did not like it at all.

He was still very angry indeed about the dance. It had been the biggest, grandest party for years – with the President of Thalassa, all the important people on the island, and fifty visitors from Earth, all at the same time.

Clyde was a good dancer, but he had little chance to show it that night. Leon had been showing everyone the

Jealousy was new to Clyde, and he did not like it at all.

latest dances from Earth (well, from a hundred years before, anyway) and in Clyde's opinion the dances were ugly and Leon was an awful dancer. He had been foolish enough to tell Lora that during one of their few dances together, and that had been his last dance with Lora that evening. From that moment on Lora neither looked at nor spoke to him, and Clyde had soon gone off to the bar to get drunk as quickly as possible. In this he was successful, and it was only the next morning that he learnt what he had missed.

The dancing had ended early. Then the President introduced the captain of the starship, who, he said, had a little surprise for everyone.

Captain Gold spoke for a short while first. He wanted, he said, to thank Thalassa for its warm welcome to the visitors from Earth. He spoke of the peace and beauty of the island, and the kindness of its people. He hoped that he and his companions would make the world that was waiting at the end of their journey as happy a home for human beings as Thalassa was. Then he went on:

'Much has happened on Earth in the three centuries since the first colonists came to Thalassa, and this is one way in which we can show our thanks to you. When we go, we can leave behind for you all the information and scientific discoveries of those years, to enrich your world in the future. But as well as science, we can leave you other things, things to delight the ear, and the heart. Listen, now, to the music from our mother Earth.'

The lights had been turned down; the music had begun. No one who was there that night ever forgot that moment, when the first strange and beautiful sounds filled the hall. Lora stood, lost in wonder, not even remembering that Leon stood by her side, holding her hand in his.

It was a music that she had never known – the sound of things that belonged to Earth, and to Earth alone. The slow beat of deep bells, the songs of patient boatmen rowing home, of armies marching into battles long ago, the whisper of ten million voices rising from the great cities, the sound of winds dancing over endless seas of ice. All these things she heard in the music, and more – the songs of distant Earth, carried to her across the light-years . . .

Then a clear high voice, rising like a bird into the sky, singing a song that went straight to every heart. It was a song for all loves lost in the loneliness of space, for friends and homes that would never be seen again, that would be forgotten for ever in years to come.

As the music died away into the darkness, the people of Thalassa, avoiding words, had gone slowly to their homes. But Lora had not gone to hers; for the loneliness that filled her heart, there was only one answer. And presently she had found it, in the warm night of the forest, as Leon's arms closed around her in the moonlight. And while the fire of love burned, they were safe from the shadows of the night and the loneliness of the stars.

*   *   *

To Leon, it was never wholly real. Sometimes he thought that at his journey's end Thalassa would seem like a dream that had come in his long sleep. This wild and desperate love, for example; he had not asked for it, but there it was.

When he could escape from work, he took long walks with Lora in the fields far from the village, where only machines worked on the land. For hours Lora would question him about Earth, wanting to know everything about the 'home' she had never seen with her own eyes.

She was very disappointed to hear that there were no longer great cities like Chandrigar or Astrograd on Earth, and that life there had changed so much since the old stories that she knew.

'But what happened to the cities?' she asked Leon.

'They disappeared for a number of reasons really,' Leon explained. 'When it became easy to see and talk to other people anywhere on Earth just by pushing a button on a computer, most of the need for cities was gone. Then we learnt how to turn off the pull of gravity, and once you can control gravity, you can move anything heavy, even houses, through the sky without difficulty. So all movement and travel became really simple. After that, people started to live where they liked, and the cities just slowly disappeared.'

Lora was lying on the grass, looking up at the sky. 'Do you suppose,' she said, 'that we'll ever break through the speed of light?'

'I don't think so,' he said smiling, knowing what she was thinking. 'We have to travel the slow way because that's how the universe is made, and there's nothing we can do about it.'

'It would be wonderful,' Lora said dreamily, 'to be able to travel back to Earth, to see what it was like, without spending hundreds of years on the journey.' But the wish would never come true, and with Leon beside her, it did not seem important. He was here; Earth and the stars were far away. And so also was tomorrow, with whatever unhappiness it would bring . . .

By the end of the week the engineers had built a strong metal pyramid on land that looked out over the sea. Lora, with the 571 other Palm Bay villagers and several thousand other Thalassans, came to watch the first test. Many of the islanders were nervous about the strange science of the visitors. Did the Earthmen know what they were doing? What if something went wrong? And *what* were they doing, anyway?

Lora knew that Leon was there inside the machine with his companions, preparing for the test. Then the engineers came out and walked to a high place where they stood, staring out to sea.

Two kilometres out, something strange was happening to the water. It looked like a storm, but a storm just in one small place. The waves grew higher and higher, then as tall as mountains, crashing wildly into each other. Suddenly, the movement changed. The waves came together, higher and thinner, and soon – to the amazement and fear of the watching Thalassans – a long river of sea water was rising *up* into the sky, climbing a hundred metres, then two, higher and higher, until it disappeared into the clouds above. Huge drops of water, escaping from the edge of the rising river, fell back down into the sea in a heavy rainstorm, but the river itself went on climbing up into space towards the starship *Magellan*.

A long river of sea water was rising up into the sky.

Slowly the crowd moved away, forgetting their first amazement and fright. Humans had been able to control gravity for many years; now they had seen it with their own eyes. A million tonnes of water from Thalassa's sea was on its way out into space, where the engineers would freeze it and shape it, and turn it into a travelling shield for the starship. In a few days the ship would be ready to leave.

Up until the last minute, Lora had hoped that they would fail. With fear in her heart, she watched the river of water rising smoothly into the sky. It meant only one thing to her; soon she must say goodbye to Leon. She walked slowly towards the group of Earthmen, trying to stay calm. Leon saw her and came to meet her, the happiness on his face turning to worry as he saw her expression.

'Well,' he said, 'we've done it.' He sounded almost ashamed, and avoided meeting her eyes.

'And now – how long will you be here?'

'Oh, about three days – perhaps four.'

Lora had expected this. She tried to speak calmly, but the words came out as a desperate cry.

'You can't leave! Stay here on Thalassa!'

Leon took her hands and said gently, 'No, Lora – this isn't my world. I've spent half my life training for the work I'm doing now. There is no work for me here, and I would be bored to death in a month.'

'Then take me with you! I would go anywhere, do anything, if we could be together!'

'You don't really mean that. You know that you would be more out of place in my world than I would be in yours.'

But as he looked into her eyes he saw that she did mean it, and for the first time he felt ashamed of himself. He had never meant to hurt her; he was very fond of her and would always remember her. Now he was discovering, as so many men before him had done, that it was not always easy to say goodbye. There was only one thing to do. Better a short, sharp pain than a long unhappiness.

'Come with me, Lora,' he said. 'I have something to show you.'

They did not speak as Leon led the way to the *Magellan*'s space bus, that great silver egg that had first brought the visitors down to Thalassa. After a short argument with another engineer there, Leon took Lora inside the bus and seconds later it had taken off, lifting smoothly into the air with no feeling of movement, no whisper of sound. Already Lora was in a world she had never known before – a world of scientific wonders that Thalassa had never needed or wanted for its life and happiness.

As Lora watched, Thalassa became just a misty curve of blue below, and soon, out of the blackness of space, the starship *Magellan* came into view. The sight of it took Lora's breath away – an endless curving wall of metal, perhaps as much as four kilometres long.

The bus found its own way home and locked itself into an entrance gate in the side of the ship. Lora followed Leon through the doors of the airlock, then stepped on to a long, moving walkway which carried them smoothly and silently into the heart of the ship.

For an hour Leon showed Lora the *Magellan*. They travelled along endless fast-moving walkways, upwards through tunnels where there was no gravity, in and out of every part of the great ship – through the engine room a kilometre long, past long rows of mysterious computers and strange machines, through huge libraries filled with every piece of information that anyone could want. The *Magellan* was a man-made and self-contained world, waiting to bring human life to a young planet far away in space. And Lora knew that Leon was showing her just how different his life was from hers.

Now they came to a great white door which slid silently open as they came near it. Inside were rows of long warm coats. Leon helped Lora to climb into one of these, and put one on himself. Then he opened a glass door in the floor, turned to her and said, 'There's no gravity down here, so keep close to me and do exactly as I say.'

Through the open door a cloud of freezing cold air was rising. Lora trembled in fear and wonder, and Leon took her arm. 'Don't worry,' he said. 'You won't notice the cold.' Then he went down through the door and Lora followed him.

Without the pull of gravity, Lora felt she was swimming, but through air rather than water. All around her, in this frozen white universe, were rows and rows of shining glass boxes, each box large enough to hold a human being.

And each box did. There they were, the thousands, tens of thousands of colonists on their way to a new world, sleeping in suspended animation until the day of their arrival. What were they dreaming in their three-hundred-year sleep? Did they dream at all in that half-world between life and death?

Overhead there were moving belts with handholds every

few metres. Leon took hold of one of these and it pulled him and Lora along past the endless rows of glass boxes. They went on and on, changing from one moving belt to another, until at last Leon let go and they came to a stop beside one box no different from all the thousands of others.

But as Lora saw Leon's expression, she knew why he had brought her here, and knew that her battle was already lost.

For a long time, unconscious of the cold, Lora stared down at the sleeping woman in her glass box, a woman who would only wake long after Lora was dead. It was not a beautiful face, but it was strong, intelligent, full of character – the face of somebody able to build a new Earth beyond the stars.

At last Lora spoke, her voice a whisper in the frozen stillness.

'Is she your wife?'

'Yes. I'm sorry, Lora. I never meant to hurt you. . .'

'It doesn't matter now. It was my fault, too.' She paused and looked more closely at the sleeping woman. 'And your child as well?'

'Yes. It will be born three months after we land.'

How strange, Lora thought, to carry a child inside you for nine months and three hundred years! But that was just another part of this strange world, Leon's world, a world that had no place for her. She knew that now, and knew that the coldness that had entered her heart would stay with her long after she had left this frozen place.

Lora stared down at the sleeping woman in her glass box.

She remembered nothing of the journey back to the space bus. Leon did something to the controls, and turned to her.

'Goodbye, Lora,' he said. 'My work is done. It would be better if I stayed here on the starship.' There were no more words to say, and Lora could not even see his face through her tears.

He took her hands in his and held them hard. 'Oh Lora,' he whispered. Then he was gone.

After what seemed like a lifetime later, Lora heard an automatic voice coming from the control board. 'We have landed; please leave by the front doors.' The doors opened and Lora went through them and down the steps outside.

Surprisingly, a small crowd was watching her arrival with interest. For a moment she did not understand why; then Clyde's voice shouted, 'Where is he?' He jumped forward, his face red with anger, and caught Lora by the arm. 'Tell him to come out and meet me like a man.'

Lora shook her head tiredly. 'He's not here. I've said goodbye to him. I'll never see him again.'

Clyde stared at her disbelievingly, then saw that she spoke the truth. In the same moment Lora threw herself into his arms, crying her heart out in her pain and misery. Clyde held her close; she belonged to him again, and all his anger disappeared like morning mist in the sunshine.

*   *   *

For almost fifty hours the river of water thundered upwards out of the sea into space. All the island watched, through television cameras, the making of the great ice shield that would ride ahead of the *Magellan* on its way to the stars.

The last day came and went. The Earthmen said their final goodbyes, and the silver space bus lifted off and climbed up into space. Some time later the night sky exploded into light, as the starship's great engines began to burn with the fire of a thousand suns.

Lora turned her face away from the sky and hid it against Clyde's shoulder. This was where she belonged. Clyde held her gently, loving her without words, but he knew that all the days of his life, the ghost of Leon would come between him and Lora – the ghost of a man who would be not one day older when they lay dead and buried.

Already the *Magellan* was moving across the sky along its lonely and unreturning road. The white fire of its engines seemed to burn less brightly, and now the soft golden light of the moon Selene could be seen again in the sky. A few moments later the *Magellan* was only a distant point of light, then even that disappeared into the long emptiness of space.

Lora now looked up at the empty sky. Leon had been right. The life of the starship was not for her. Her life was here, on this quiet island. The colonists of the *Magellan* belonged to the future. Leon and his companions would be moving seas, levelling mountains, and fighting unknown dangers, when her descendants in two hundred years' time would still be dreaming on the peaceful beaches of Thalassa.

And which life was better, who could say?

GLOSSARY

amazement   very great surprise

architect   a person who designs buildings

brain   the part of the head that thinks

colonist   a person who goes to another country (or planet) and makes it their home

communicate   to send information, news, ideas to other people by speaking, writing, radio, computer, etc.

curve *(n)*   a line which is not straight (e.g. like part of a circle)

descendant   a person of your family who is born a long time after you

dimension   a measurement of any kind; something flat like a piece of paper has two dimensions (long and wide) and something like a box has three dimensions (long, wide, and deep)

drunk *(adj)*   confused in the mind after drinking too much alcohol

explosive *(n)*   something like a bomb, which can explode

faint *(adj)*   not strong or clear; not easily seen

foolish   silly, not sensible or clever

fuss *(v)*   nervous excitement or unnecessary worry; opposite of calmness

God   the being whom some people believe made the universe

gravity   the force that on Earth pulls things towards the centre of the planet, so that things fall to the ground when dropped

hallucination   something which you think you see or hear but which isn't actually there

hamster   a small animal like a rat or a mouse

handkerchief   a small square of cloth for blowing your nose into, etc.

horizon the line at which the land and sky seem to meet

huge very, very big

invent to make or think of something that is completely new

joke *(n)* something done or said to cause amusement or laughter

laboratory a room or building used for scientific research

lama a holy man belonging to the Buddhist religion

mathematician a person who studies mathematics, the science of numbers

mayor the chief official in a town or village

mind *(n)* the part of a person that thinks, feels, remembers, etc.

monastery a building in which monks or other holy people live together as a group

nervous worried and afraid

planet Earth is one of the nine planets that move around our sun

point *(v)* to show with the arm or finger where something is

prayer a message, spoken or silent, that you send to God

print *(v)* to put words on paper with a machine (e.g. to print a book)

purpose the reason or plan for something you want to do

puzzled unable to understand

pyramid a building or shape that is square at the bottom, with four sides that go up and meet in a point at the top

research *(n)* detailed study in order to discover new facts or information

rocket a machine that drives a spaceship up into and through space

science the study of all natural things (e.g. physics, biology are sciences)

scientist somebody who studies or works with one of the sciences

sequence numbers, actions, etc. that follow each other in a special or regular way

shield something (e.g. a piece of glass or metal) that stops something else from getting damaged

space   the sky and everything beyond it, to the last star

strip (*n*)   a long narrow piece of paper, material, land, etc.

surface   the outside of something, e.g. a box has six surfaces

suspended animation   being alive but not conscious

telepathic   being able to communicate directly from one mind to
   another without speaking

theodolite   something used (e.g. in making maps) to measure
   how high or far away something is

tool   an instrument; something held in the hand and used for
   working on something (e.g. a hammer or screwdriver)

tunnel   an underground passage for a road or railway

twist (*n*)   something which is not straight

universe   the Earth and all the stars, planets, etc. in space

wise   knowing many things and having or showing good
   judgement

The Songs of Distant Earth
and Other Stories

ACTIVITIES

ACTIVITIES

Before Reading

1 **Read the back cover and the introduction on the first page of the book. What do you know now about these stories? Choose T (true) or F (false) for each sentence.**

1 Scientists on the Moon discover some alarming information. T/F

2 Bill Cross sends a warning to the planet Thaar. T/F

3 The planet Thaar is five hundred miles away from Earth. T/F

4 Tibetan lamas believe that there are less than nine million names for God. T/F

5 Shervane lives in a part of the Universe which is a long way from Earth. T/F

6 Lora and Clyde have never lived on Earth. T/F

7 The starship *Magellan* often makes the journey from Earth to Thalassa. T/F

2 **How long is a light-year? Do you know, or can you guess? Choose one of these answers.**

A light-year is the distance that light travels in one year, which is about . . .

1 five and a half million km. (5,500,000 km)

2 nine thousand million km. (9,000,000,000 km)

3 six and a half million million km. (6,500,000,000,000 km)

4 nine and a half million million km. (9,500,000,000,000 km)

3 **Can you guess what will happen in the stories? Choose endings for each of these sentences. (You can choose more than one if you like.)**

1 The Tibetan lamas' search for God's names leads to . . .

a) war and fighting between every country in the world.

b) the appearance of God on Earth.

c) peace and understanding between all human beings.

d) the end of the universe.

2 The terrible secret discovered on the Moon is . . .

a) about how long human beings can live.

b) a new disease which will kill most humans.

c) a new deadly weapon invented by people on Mars.

d) about the Earth becoming too hot for human life.

3 The Wall of Darkness . . .

a) is an imaginary wall that is only in Shervane's mind.

b) sends Shervane mad.

c) is a real wall, but with something very strange about it.

d) can only be crossed with the help of God.

4 The warning from the planet Thaar is . . .

a) about the end of the universe.

b) a personal warning for Bill Cross.

c) about danger for the planet Earth.

d) about Thaar's plan to destroy Earth.

5 On the planet Thalassa, Lora . . .

a) decides to travel to Earth on the starship *Magellan*.

b) falls in love with someone from the starship *Magellan*.

c) learns that Earth has been destroyed.

d) dreams that she is living on Earth.

ACTIVITIES

While Reading

Read *The Nine Billion Names of God*. Are these sentences true
(T) or false (F)? Rewrite the false ones with the correct
information.

1 Lamas in Tibet were trying to list all God's names.
2 The names were written in the Greek alphabet.
3 They had been working on this list for fifteen thousand
   years and it would take another three centuries to finish it.
4 The computer could do this work in about three months.
5 Chuck and George found out the reason for making this
   list, and they believed it was true.
6 They arranged a breakdown so that they could stay.
7 The lamas were wrong about God's purpose, and when
   the list was complete, nothing happened.

Read *The Secret*, and then answer these questions.

Why

1 ... was Henry Cooper chosen by UNSA to go to the
   Moon?
2 ... did Cooper phone the Chief Inspector?
3 ... was Chandra also worried about the Medical Group?
4 ... did Dr Hastings agree to meet Cooper?
5 ... was a ten-year-old hamster surprising?
6 ... would the news about life on the Moon be a problem?
7 ... couldn't everybody go to live on the Moon?

Read *The Wall of Darkness*. This summary is full of mistakes. Rewrite the passage with the correct information.

Shervane lived in a universe with many planets. The great mystery of his world was the Wall of Darkness, but Shervane did not want to find out its secret. When he and Brayldon first went to look at the Wall, it was not as strange as they had expected. The Wall was made of metal, and they were able to cut and mark the surface with their tools.

Years later, they built a great stairway up both sides of the Wall. Shervane went up to the top with Brayldon, and then walked in a straight line across the top of the wall, keeping Trilorne in front of him. He was pleased when he arrived back at exactly the same place he had started from.

To explain this strangeness, Grayle showed Brayldon how a piece of wood could become a three-sided surface. This was an example in three dimensions of what must happen in two dimensions at the Wall. So the Wall, Grayle thought, had been built to send people mad.

Read *No Morning After*, and answer these questions.

1 What were the two things that made it difficult for the Thaarns to communicate their message to Earth?
2 Why was Bill drunk?
3 What did Bill think the misty tunnel was?
4 What would happen if Bill stepped into the tunnel?
5 Why didn't Bill want to accept the Thaarns' offer of help?
6 Why did Bill forget about the warning for three days?
7 Why wasn't there a fourth day?

Read *The Songs of Distant Earth* down to the end of page 61. How do you think the story will end? Choose Y (yes) or N (no) for each of these ideas.

1 Lora wants to leave with Leon on the *Magellan*. Y/N
2 Clyde has a fight with Leon, and Leon is badly hurt. Y/N
3 Leon asks Lora to go with him on the *Magellan*. Y/N
4 Lora learns that Leon is already married. Y/N
5 Leon leaves Thalassa, Lora stays, and marries Clyde. Y/N
6 Leon stays on Thalassa, and marries Lora. Y/N

Read the rest of the story, and join these parts of sentences.

1 Leon had never meant to hurt Lora and felt ashamed . . .
2 He did not want to stay on Thalassa . . .
3 So he took Lora up to the *Magellan* . . .
4 When Lora saw the sleeping woman in the glass box, . . .
5 She realized then that she had lost the battle . . .
6 But as she watched the starship leaving a few days later, . . .

7 and showed her the real reason . . .
8 she knew that Thalassa was . . .
9 when he realized . . .
10 and that there was no place for her in Leon's world.
11 why she couldn't go with him on the starship's journey.
12 where she really belonged.
13 how much she cared about him.
14 she guessed at once who she was.
15 because he knew he would be bored with a quiet life.

ACTIVITIES

After Reading

1 Perhaps this is what some of the characters in the stories were thinking. Which characters were they (one from each story), and what had just happened in the story?

1 'No, close down the contact now. There's no point in continuing. You've done your best, but clearly he either can't, or won't, understand us. So there's nothing we can do to help these poor humans . . .'

2 'I know those footsteps. Good. Now we can talk. Perhaps he has guessed the truth already. If not, I'll explain it to him. I'll need some paper – yes, I've got some here . . .'

3 'I suppose he's right – I *will* have to talk to this reporter. Better he hears it from me than from someone else. I just hope he understands what trouble this news could cause if it got out . . .'

4 'Oh, my head does hurt! But what else was there to do last night, except drink? She wouldn't even look at me – too busy dancing with that engineer. And I missed the singing too. Everyone's talking about it – I wish I'd heard it . . .'

5 'So, they have gone. I can see them riding down the path. I knew they wanted to get away before the end. But it's not important. Everything is running smoothly, and God's purpose will soon be finished . . .'

2 Here is a page from Chuck's diary. Complete it, using the
   words below (one word for each gap).

   complete, computer, crazier, craziest, crazy, end, endless,
   meaningless, monastery, nervous, possibly, universe, world

   This is the _____ job I've ever been on. Here we are, in a
   _____ half-way up a mountain, with a _____ printing out an
   _____ list of _____ names. But what's even _____ is this –
   poor old Sam thinks that when the list is _____, it'll be the
   _____, not just of our _____, but of the whole _____. It's a
   _____ idea, of course it is. So why do I feel so _____? They
   can't _____ be right . . . can they?

3 After his meeting with Dr Hastings, Henry Cooper (in *The*
   Secret) writes a report for Earth. Choose seven of these ten
   linking words to complete his report.

   because / but / how / however / than / that / what / which /
   who / why

   Medical researchers here have been studying the effects _____
   the Moon's gravity has on the human body. Fighting Earth's
   gravity is hard work for the body, _____ here it has to do
   only a sixth of that work _____ on the Moon the body weighs
   much less. This means that the body will be able to live much
   longer _____ it can in Earth's gravity. The effect on hamsters,
   _____ normally live for two years, is that they will have a life
   of about ten years on the Moon. _____, a much greater effect
   on the length of life will be seen in human beings, _____ can
   expect to live for at least two hundred years.

4 Do you think Henry Cooper sent his report – or did he destroy it, and keep the secret? What would *you* do?

5 What did Shervane say to Brayldon after his walk across the Wall of Darkness? Put their conversation in the right order, and write in the speakers' names. Begin with number 4.

  1 _____ 'No. I went on walking, with my back to Trilorne. And then Trilorne appeared again, *in front of me.*'

  2 _____ 'But there must be! Where did you go?'

  3 _____ 'Impossible, but it happened. And that's why, Brayldon, we must now destroy our stairway.'

  4 _____ 'What did you find on the other side, Shervane?'

  5 _____ 'I walked in a straight line across the wall, and arrived back here, where I started.'

  6 _____ 'In front of you? That's impossible, surely?'

  7 _____ 'Nothing, Brayldon. There *is* no other side.'

  8 _____ 'A straight line? You didn't turn left or right?'

6 How did Grayle explain the idea of a one-sided surface? Follow these instructions and try it yourself.

  1 Take a strip of paper about 30 cm long and 2 cm wide.

  2 Give one end a half-turn (180°) so that the strip has a twist in it, then join the two ends together.

  3 With a pen draw a line down the centre of the strip, without taking your pen off the paper, and continue drawing until you meet the place where you started.

What is surprising about the line you have drawn?

7 Imagine that Bill (in *No Morning After*) decided to phone the
   president about the Thaarns' warning. What did he say?
   Complete the conversation (use as many words as you like).

BILL: _____
PRESIDENT: I'm listening, Dr Cross. What kind of message?
BILL: _____
PRESIDENT: As far as *Jupiter*? Who gave you this warning?
BILL: _____
PRESIDENT: Another *planet*? And just how did these scientists
   from another planet get this warning to you, Dr Cross?
BILL: _____
PRESIDENT: Oh, I see. They want to help us, do they? How?
BILL: _____
PRESIDENT: The thirty-seventh *what*?! Listen, Dr Cross, I'm a
   busy man. I don't have time for crazy jokes. Goodbye!

8 Use the notes to write a paragraph for each of these different
   endings for *The Songs of Distant Earth*. Which ending do you
   prefer – one of these, or the one in the story? Explain why.

   1 Leon decided to stay on Thalassa . . .
      wrong thing / bored / argued with Lora / Lora unhappy /
      went back to Clyde / married / Leon sad, lonely
   2 Leon decided to stay on Thalassa . . .
      married Lora / fisherman / simple, peaceful life / Clyde
      unhappy / married someone else / everybody happy
   3 Lora left with Leon on the *Magellan* . . .
      200 years suspended animation / new planet / life difficult,
      dangerous / Lora hated / unhappy / wished / Thalassa

9 Here are some different titles for the stories. Which titles go with which stories? Which titles do you like best? Put them in order for each story, with the best first, and the worst last.

- Warning from Thaar
- News from Plato City
- Starship from Earth
- No Other Side
- Himalayan Adventure
- The Long Sleep
- Love on a Far Planet
- The Stars Go Out
- A Twist in the Universe
- A Human Life

- Death of the Sun
- Horizon's End
- The Hallucination
- An Unwise List
- Beyond the Shadow Land
- The Last Ride
- The Moon Problem
- Journey to the Stars
- Humans and Hamsters
- The Whisky Dimension

10 If, one day, human life on Earth came to an end, what would be the most probable cause, in your opinion? Put these ideas in order of probability. Can you think of any other causes?

1 Human beings go to live on other planets in the universe.
2 The sun explodes and destroys Earth.
3 God decides to punish human beings.
4 There is a world war, with terrible modern weapons.
5 A large object from outer space (like a meteor) hits Earth.
6 Beings from another planet attack Earth.
7 The sun gets too hot, the seas dry up, and all the trees die.
8 There is a new, terrible disease which kills all humans.

11 Which of the five stories in this book did you like best, and which one could you *nearly* believe? Why?

ABOUT THE AUTHOR

Arthur Charles Clarke was born in 1917 in Somerset, England. From an early age he was interested in everything scientific, building his own wireless sets, telescopes to look at the moon, and several home-made rockets. He was also an enthusiastic reader and collector of science-fiction magazines. From 1941 to 1946 he served in the Royal Air Force as a Technical Officer, and in 1945 he published an article which predicted the development of communications satellites – many of which are fixed in the geostationary orbit 36,000 kilometres above the equator, known as the Clarke Ring. In 1946 he published his first science-fiction short story, and two years later gained a degree in physics and mathematics from London University. He travelled widely, published several successful novels, and became a keen deep-sea diver. Since 1956 he has lived in Colombo, Sri Lanka, in a house full of computers and all kinds of modern electronic technology.

Arthur C. Clarke has lectured in Britain and the United States, has made many radio and television appearances, and has written about eighty books and five hundred articles and short stories. He has received countless awards, and is famous both for his science writing – on space flight, scientific forecasting, and undersea exploration – and for his inventive and technologically detailed science fiction.

Some of his best-known titles are the short stories 'The Sentinel', 'The Star', 'Transit of Earth', and 'The Nine Billion Names of God'. His many successful novels include *Childhood's End* (1953), *Rendezvous with Rama* (1973), and *Imperial Earth* (1975).

His greatest success is probably *2001: A Space Odyssey* (1968) – he wrote the novel and co-authored the screenplay for the famous Stanley Kubrick film.

All his life Arthur C. Clarke has had a deep interest in the meeting point between science and science fiction. Many of his predictions have come true, and what is fiction today might easily become the fact of tomorrow. A book he published in 1962 included his Three Laws, which are:

The First Law: 'When a distinguished but elderly scientist says that something is possible, he is almost certainly right. When he says it is impossible, he is very probably wrong.'

The Second Law: 'The only way to find the limits of the possible is by going beyond them into the impossible.'

The Third Law: 'Any sufficiently advanced technology is indistinguishable from magic.'

ABOUT BOOKWORMS

OXFORD BOOKWORMS LIBRARY
*Classics • True Stories • Fantasy & Horror • Human Interest
Crime & Mystery • Thriller & Adventure*

The OXFORD BOOKWORMS LIBRARY offers a wide range of original and adapted stories, both classic and modern, which take learners from elementary to advanced level through six carefully graded language stages:

Stage 1 (400 headwords)	**Stage 4** (1400 headwords)
Stage 2 (700 headwords)	**Stage 5** (1800 headwords)
Stage 3 (1000 headwords)	**Stage 6** (2500 headwords)

More than fifty titles are also available on cassette, and there are many titles at Stages 1 to 4 which are specially recommended for younger learners. In addition to the introductions and activities in each Bookworm, resource material includes photocopiable test worksheets and Teacher's Handbooks, which contain advice on running a class library and using cassettes, and the answers for the activities in the books.

Several other series are linked to the OXFORD BOOKWORMS LIBRARY. They range from highly illustrated readers for young learners, to playscripts, non-fiction readers, and unsimplified texts for advanced learners.

Oxford Bookworms Starters   *Oxford Bookworms Factfiles*
Oxford Bookworms Playscripts   *Oxford Bookworms Collection*

Details of these series and a full list of all titles in the OXFORD BOOKWORMS LIBRARY can be found in the *Oxford English* catalogues. A selection of titles from the OXFORD BOOKWORMS LIBRARY can be found on the next pages.

BOOKWORMS • FANTASY &. HORROR • STAGE 4
Dr Jekyll and Mr Hyde
ROBERT LOUIS STEVENSON
Retold by Rosemary Border

You are walking through the streets of London. It is getting dark and you want to get home quickly. You enter a narrow side-street. Everything is quiet, but as you pass the door of a large, windowless building, you hear a key turning in the lock. A man comes out and looks at you. You have never seen him before, but you realize immediately that he hates you. You are shocked to discover, also, that you hate him.

Who is this man that everybody hates? And why is he coming out of the laboratory of the very respectable Dr Jekyll?

BOOKWORMS • FANTASY & HORROR • STAGE 5
I, Robot
ISAAC ASIMOV
Retold by Rowena Akinyemi

A human being is a soft, weak creature. It needs constant supplies of air, water, and food; it has to spend a third of its life asleep, and it can't work if the temperature is too hot or too cold.

But a robot is made of strong metal. It uses electrical energy directly, never sleeps, and can work in any temperature. It is stronger, more efficient – and sometimes more human than human beings.

Isaac Asimov was one of the greatest science-fiction writers, and these short stories give us an unforgettable and terrifying vision of the future.

BOOKWORMS • FANTASY & HORROR • STAGE 4

The Unquiet Grave

M. R. JAMES

Retold by Peter Hawkins

If you find a locked room in a lonely inn, don't try to open it, even on a bright sunny day. If you find a strange whistle hidden among the stones of an old church, don't blow it. If a mysterious man gives you a piece of paper with strange writing on it, give it back to him at once. And if you call a dead man from his grave, don't expect to sleep peacefully ever again.

Read these five ghost stories by daylight, and make sure your door is locked.

BOOKWORMS • FANTASY & HORROR • STAGE 5

Do Androids Dream of Electric Sheep?

PHILIP K. DICK

Retold by Andy Hopkins and Joc Potter

San Francisco lies under a cloud of radioactive dust. People live in half-deserted apartment buildings, and keep electric animals as pets because so many real animals have died. Most people emigrate to Mars – unless they have a job to do on Earth.

Like Rick Deckard – android killer for the police and owner of an electric sheep. This week he has to find, identify, and kill six androids which have escaped from Mars. They're machines, but they look and sound and think like humans – clever, dangerous humans. They will be hard to kill.

The film *Blade Runner* was based on this famous novel.